Distilled in Song

Poems by

Pat Barber

Research Associates and Publishers:
Drew Gillum & Kevin Acers

ISBN-13: 9798575143468

Printed in the United States of America

CONTENTS

FORWARD

I kept thinking about this or that favorite poem I had saved for its practical ideas and inspiration, for its sometimes pungent turns of phrase that brought me a clear new meaning about the offices of wife and mother, of husband, father, and child, of their interaction, and interdependency on God. I hope that the objective, hard-earned dimensions of these poems will companion usefully with your own vigorous and precious family work.

Pat Barber
December 2020

Distilled in Song

WELCOME

None home but me, I see.
I enter the close silence
of the empty house and miss
voices and noise. But still
there is a presence here
poised at the point of fullness.

Home.   A presence itself...

That is it: *home*, usefully loved.   That,
and the fur-stretched, sleeping cat.

THE LIGHT THAT BOUNCES

is best: that rebounds
off grass blades as sword-bling
and walls as warmth;

that pings
off dust motes
as confetti-float,
and butterflies
as engined gleams;

that dazzles off of birdflight
as slip-glide glory
and a spider's orb
as crystal cipher;

that shimmers off waves
as coruscating laugh,
off the face, as *am*,
and off the crown of the head as *have*.

ROBIN, NOTED WITH INTEREST

She fed winter-wise on the ground
about the feeder; breasted snow-flung
winds, and sang at dawn, bound
to wait the winter out and grow young
in spring. And she has. The oaks
are barely budded above the red
of redbud trees, and she pokes
mud among the twigs and thread
gleaned from the neighborhood
to furnish out her high-crotched nest.
The sight of her feathered love is good
for us, part of spring's busy rest
from winter. Her early treetop invasion,
amidst wars and rumors of wars, is a signal occasion.

DAY BEFORE WINTER

How cradled the earth appears with clouds, how soft

under oblique sun; how gentled down the pastel

grass—how poised for change, how meek is everything,

how loved! The slight, receding sun

has breathed a summer sigh clear into November.

The trees are drained to muted colors. Still

streams lie pooled in dreams set in

before the hills have wintered down to snow

and seedheads glow with warm-day tints,

round with hints of purpose. Those pasture grasses

will hold the light ground-shining into night.

When the sun slants too far for green,

this mitigating day will have been art enough

to keep the heart ardent with this lean loveliness.

JOY RIDE

The earth turns toward the set

center of our galaxy, and we

are on the brink

of day. Dawn never seemed

so welcome, movement toward

the central light and certain

warmth so playful. It is our turn,

China. You may stargaze now and let

the moon shine poetic rest

while we incline sunward

and sing with dawn-fire zest!

LETTER TO A FRIEND IN ALASKA

Weather-clawed, your monowhite
winter drags a dreary rake, and fierce!

How can I help pierce your gloom? How
can I share this tabletop of roses with you

       comfort of a Cezanne summer
       a Dufy spring

and you so far away? Not even a camera
is enough to bring you their totality of presence

       a warm horde
       of glory that belies

the snowy winter skies of which you write
gone daytime-dark and blizzard-bold.

Today may end our autumn; tonight will hold
a freeze, the weatherman supposes.
Well, we have this bouquet

> and the knowing about
> roses,
> roses' glow.

So, I send that herewith:

> the *knowing*,

guaranteed perfect against
any arctic air. And you have that,

> the knowing

already with you, already there.
What fun this be:
to give you what you already have

> without redundancy!

WINTER'S PART

It is the simplicity that endears this season
to the heart weathered to love the part winter
plays in the year: clear of spring adornment,
of summer or fall festoon, winter is color-
quiet and petalfree, remote of sun,
with cold-metal moon.
                                    It is wise-open to new
meanings: its gleanings rest at nadir, cupped:
its stern virtues cradle the nascent *now*:
now is the time for fireplace glow within,
paw-print snow without; for slow thaws
and raw freeze, for crunch and drift
and hidden life; now is the time to treasure
covenant skies and Euclidean trees
beauty-bare in a zero-welded air
that holds fruit-tending buds from untimely
breaking.
                    Making no wish for another, better
season, now is the time to measure
deep through the woods the horizon's bright raven,
patient on the wing; to cling to and savor
this sabbath of the seasons as haven, as stave—
the year's nimbus, nexus, nidus, nave.

NOTICED ABOUT MY PARENTS

Marriage of true hearts weathers wonders
and woes: it is winged with moral law:
rooted, engined, lifted, and buoyed
with the Golden Rule.

It is not neat: it is uphill-downdale
constant self-correction. It is shed-the-outgrown,
unfold-the-new. It is give and give.

It is governing oneself
and thereby the sullen cloud, the unruly storm.

It is the work and play of teamed heroes
through domesticities or danger—cosy
as a clover patch, demanding as high tide.

It is the comfort of touch,
the assurance of space
apart. It is love seasoned to grace,
lithe with the essential striving trim
which can last through fire
                              or ice.

It is two devoted to the oneness
that embraces both: it warms to inclusiveness,
ripens to permanence.

It is sapling commitment
to columnar fidelity.

WHAT THE WHOLE UNIVERSE JUST LOVES:

the regal littleness

of snail carapaced

with spiral shell

and furnished

with tenderest

slick of single foot.

AUTUMN'S HONORS

This year
the leaves prepared for disengagement
by turning shocking orange and mocking
the yellow of the chrysanthemum.
They left the trees by ones and twenty-threes
to re-amass on the grass and around
the ground under the marigolds and shrubs.
                              So that now
the house is banked isolate with leaves
that insulate blooms of rust and purple, bronze
and gold, against November's advance of cold
in undulate drifts of protection,
                                    while oak and
hackberry leaves by the score whirl through the door
with zephyr-footed guests and defy ejection
by clinging to cuffs, heels, carpet and broom.
                              Into every room
they come—in the pockets and socks and sweaters
of the children who have run inside fresh
from the theme-and-variation of leaf-wallowing—
dusty-pungent, crisp-colored, tenacious.

So it is all fall,
outside and in, in the air and under feet:
leafy confetti to celebrate child's play, the late-day
flowers, and visitor's call. Not neat. But somehow
                              gracious.

READY, SET,
CONVERGE

The cat's success
at fine-tuning felicity
is succinct

a contemplation
concisely upright

breath a brevity
of wound-down purr

intently compact
claws in retract
unblinkingly still
(skies in his eyes)
on the windowsill

ears at alert
whiskers pert with light
fur tips terse
tail tucked tight
to hold contentment
and the whole, tall
sinewy precision of it all
taut.

SHEER TO LIGHT

There are days
        (early spring and sudden,
        at the fell end of fall,
        poise of midsummer)
when butterflies
fly single
and seem the size
of dinner plates
they dominate the landscape so.

        Serene
they beat the sustaining delay of air,
pulsating summer essence outward
in waves beneficent and multiplied,
        suncasts gone sheer to light
        like plants to seed.

Knowing no caterpillar need nor chrysalis past,
no vein-shattered, pollen-scattered wings
brittled by winter-blast indifference,
they are butterfly-life wholly:

against every educated evidence a foreverness,

a death-denying
high-summer consciousness
        unimperiled:

an evocation
        hardy
        and perennial.

CONTINUUM

Now cause for smiles
the self-made miles of no-further
accepted once by those
who saw the earth
flat. And so it goes—we are
well-served to see beyond seeing
empty space, and nerved to aspire
to light-years of go-higher
with the lesson in grace and verve
that, like the earth,
space includes the comfort of curve
for men to extend and enter;
while curve implies full circle—
and circle, sure center.

NATURE QUALITATIVE

SCIENCE. Comprehension of truth, understanding;
a method and an attitude...a particular kind of
activity and also the results of that activity.
                        -*The New Columbia Encyclopedia*

Nature qualitative knows no mediocrity—
not in any random leaf nor stray
stone or fixed star; knows no
shabbiness of shoal or frond, waterfall
or particle, pinion, or leap and lap
of miles-long wave; lavishes
excellence on the foam's bubble, the cricket's
lacquered song; refines space with rainbows'
silken colors, flings precisions of crystal
within the earth and brings prismatic brilliances
to brim in mountain-spill abundance.

Splendor shimmers everywhere: iridescent snail,
breaching blue whale, eagle's exactitudes
of soar and wheel and stall, fruited and vestal
folds of land unaccidental in purpose. Nature
beyond nature empowers all its parts with
wholeness unredundant, endows each
with unique estate; defines itself
uncarnivorous, innocent, unopposed:
commissions creation an always-dawning
dearness—
hold and stronghold of men's sounding,
tideflow,
lawful, artful, single, scientific heart.

LETTER OF (URGENT) RECOMMENDATION

To the director of the next space shuttle,
on behalf of my son

Dear Sir: These times stir
fresh fires of ambition and here is one
abounding boy wishing to orbit the earth
or circle the moon. Soon! His desires press
immediacy, and if not tomorrow, then in June,
please, when kindergarten is over. Gravitationless
glory seems common, everyday-logical
to this astrohappy rover, this rocket-thoughted
lad, this in-his-own-skyey-eyes Man of Flight.

In all honesty, however, I must add...

about this applicant-hero, this brother to stars
and lover of far sweeps of flotation all outer
space: he might like a little nightlight
out there to shine upon his home-reflecting face.

IN PRAISE OF MEANS IN LINE WITH ENDS

Autumn has softened to pearl-oyster and liquid
gray: I like the sopping-wet of it, don't
you? this ancient moisture to breathe, walk
on and through?
                          The grass to its deeps is steeped
in ant-eyed dew from days hanging
clouds solid-sky-down in grays
like wet paint on wet watercolor paper.
Our water planet orbit-hugs its fire-moved
vapors:
              restraint of droplets beads each
tree, bush, blade, tip of squirrel's
fur: collects and rolls away one by
one by millions.
                          How new-given-unto
we are the way this venerable rain fills
our fall full: not by buckets dashed
nor driven by willful wind, but washed on—
thinned—into genial atmosphere;
                                        as distilled
as compassion, this cosmic cradling of seeds, lambs,
doves and children—these still waters for every one.

Its gentleness magnifies gentleness and will dry
luminous later under the circled, certain sun.

GALAXIES OBSERVED

The report is in
that when electrons spin at speeds
near that of light
        and are guided
by a magnetic field,
they yield up light
        and noise,
                    and so do galaxies:

                Oh luminous space
                and sounding speed
of pinwheel poise and lullaby. Mt. Wilson
and Palomar verify
the ancient, uninstrumented intuitions
        ...in thy light shall we
        see light
        and,—he who listens, hears—
the music of the spheres.

NEITHER X NOR ICE

"Stellar Chlorophyll Discovered
  in Outer Space"   —News Item

Stellar dust, once feared
inimical to man and life,
is now believed to be
the solid molecular stuff
that plants are made of.
So neither X nor ice
fills space, but a familiar
part of green and growing
things, and men who dream
of alien worlds or galaxy-
visit will surely be at home
with this interstellar dew—
element of apple leaves,
and grass, and heavenly bamboo.

SATURDAY MORNING HAPPINESS

has a long history
with me; goes back to childhood waking
in a yellow room with tall, father-built toy
shelves with a tea set tiny on a shelf
by itself and a spent musical top, jacks
and prized golf ball, a frayed jump rope
humming teddybear-teddybear—and sun
scintillating in the south window sideways
and reverberating around that yellow-on-yellow
room like tomorrow's hymns.

It is waking
to bed-level windows curtained
with white sheers
and open-full of night
strains of air caught
shadow-cool under foundation shrubs, and mingling
with the sun-warmed strands of barely-spring-green-
grass-odors and masses of great, plump lilac blooms
on old bushes all health and hearty leaves
and background to our young mother
hanging laundry on a line and smiling
back at the lilacs and back to our bedroom, letting
sleeping puppies lie, and somehow the reason
the lilacs were fragrant, the strawberry jam
to come so extravagantly and royally good.

It is expectation, unschooled openness.
It is the small town immediacy of people
going grocery shopping, feeding backyard chickens, waiting
for the mill's noon whistle to widen the morning
into afternoon. It is kicking off roller skates
and running inside for a lunch that tastes like gratitude,
and to hear plans that sound like wonder: a drive to
a farm friend's home for country strangenesses and
good eats ending with a freezer of ice cream
colder than dairy-bought, and richer
because of the mean little Jersey's ample cream.

But its final focus, like an evanescence
an afterimage, to this day,
is that young father's making love visible
and that young mother's pinning a family's clothes clean
against the embracing sky
for whom
the lilacs always bloom, the strawberries still ripen.

BECAUSE IT'S CENTRIFUGAL

(On hearing Scarlatti's Sonata for Harpsichord,
 G Major)

Across centuries
the ages stay in touch,
are interjoined (fore-
known/afterknown, whole):

Scarlatti's sonata-reach
breaches the obsolete
harpsichord of the seventeenth
with twentieth-plus in joy
for the adventure of order
that begets order, that pulses and tracks
      like computers or auroras
      like digital clocks
      like sunshine-conducted roses
      like careful constellations.

Scarlatti courses true to the tenor
of these times. Industry,
rocket-space, the skills
of change and bright invention
      throb through his lines,
plucked particle or struck flow,
and his percussive music
      contemporaneously shines.

DISCOVERIES: GALAXIES AND ELECTRON RINGER

Ten million light years
from earth
a galaxy forms its birth before
our instrumented eyes:
release of energy spirals out
and flies through magnitude
on magnitude—and where there was none—
                    now, M-81!

Vastnesses away,
energy akin
to five million shooting suns
is hewed to pinwheel spin and play—M-82
                    comes true,
and in galactic grace
a luminous-lovely band is released
to race for a hundred thousand years
                    to reach and ring
M-81.   And do they (sixty million
                    million
                    million
                    miles from earth)
               companionably sing
               the cosmic curve through
to a macro-minded me, a stellar-hearted you?

TO MYSELF I SAY

Spring must be raised, praised up

from under routines of keeping cosy,

rosy fires, shuttered home: routines of weathering

chipped-diamond snows, blanched earth

under rows of icicles; routines breathed through

with pent-up waiting. Trumpet time

aside, now! Bring out new things,

forgotten treasures. Mark sifting snow

as obsolete. Clear winter-littered shelves.

Dream of dark bulbs blown into blossoms.

Count robins, discount cold. Boldly

anticipate fragrances. Finger seed catalogues,

cast forth saved seeds. Let faith

burn, fervor surge—unbuckle winter!

Like a vine-traveling Tarzan, sure of the trail,

certain of the destination, swing

by day-links into spring. Hang joy

in swags about the house. Rouse sleeping strains

of song that ring echoes off a frozen

sky and multiply melt to a shimmer. Bring

happiness to a simmer. Simplify.

Spring seeks its stride in us, mid-snows,

before sap wells up or first crocus shows.

BEYOND WINTER

There are days
            (early spring and sudden,
            at the fell end of fall,
            poise of midsummer)
when butterflies
fly single
and seem the size
of dinner plates
they dominate the landscape so.

            Serene
they smite the sustaining resist of air,
pulsating summer essence outward
in waves beneficent and multiplied,
            suncasts gone sheer to light
            like plants to seed.

Knowing no caterpillar need nor chrysalis past,
no vein-shattered, pollen-scattered wings
brittled by winter-blast indifference,
they are butterfly-life wholly:

against every educated evidence a foreverness,

a death-denying
high-summer consciousness
            unimperiled:

an evocation
            hardy
            and perennial.

SMALL-TOWN GIRL

My father married a small town
replete in this girl of the purple-blue eyes
who pledged him her troth, that troth consisting
of an unremitting Irish jealousy
and small-town judgements that made her keep
a clean house, go to church on Sundays,
and prefer to be caught dead than to wear
a red dress or ankle-strap shoes.
She blamed the woman or the Other Woman in any
divorce as though it were laid-down law,
kept her girls' hair braided
awesomely tight, their clothes immaculate
from the Maytag wringer and ironed stiff
enough to repel all criticism and attract
only the Best as friends.

All this

while she herself marched constant guard
against all the Other Women
who might be after my bewildered father
who had all he could handle in her
and who could hardly imagine an Other Woman.
All that time, for all those years,
she would rather have been reading
paperback novels the livelong day
and dancing every night under an April moon
with apple blossoms mashed against her breast
by my father gone romantic, herself
in red ankle-straps hidden by a long
white dress, and forever and ever eighteen.

THE STONE THE BUILDERS REJECTED

Humility,
waking to the presence
of infinity
with a willing heart,
looks away from the proud disparity
of mortal sense
and finds the clarity
of Soul,
revealing man's true science and art
now Genesis-simple, Christ pure here
and whole!

ANNIVERSARY

Marriage of true hearts defies time's threats:
it is winged with moral law:
rooted, engined, lifted, and buoyed
with the Golden Rule.

It is not neat: it is uphill-downdale
constant self-correction. It is shed-the-outgrown,
unfold-the-new. It is give and give.
It is governing oneself
and thereby the sullen cloud, the unruly storm.

It is the work and play of teamed heroes
through domesticities or danger—cosy
as a clover patch, demanding as high tide.

It is the comfort of touch,
the assurance of space
apart. It is love seasoned to grace,
lithe with the essential striving trim
which can last through fire

                              or ice.
It is two devoted to the oneness
that embraces both: it warms to inclusiveness,
ripens to permanence.

It is sapling commitment
transforming to columnar fidelity.

NOTICED ABOUT
MY MOTHER-IN-LAW

She is duty's daughter—
a sinewy mother-lovesong
that holds hard
to her soft sympathy
each child and each child's
child. She
worth-whiles each day
away in work
               and play (her laugh
a bubble's splash of rainbow).
Her serving
strong as stainless steel
in polished practice goes,
and on her hands
every knuckle is a rose.

THE GREATER

"Photograph taken at Mt. Wilson and Palomar
Observatories gives glimpse of birth process
of a great galaxy of stars." —News Item

Yesterday's universe
shines about our earth's today,
it appears, when we receive
a picture from steep upper space
of a galaxy of stars forming
someplace ten million years
ago—the light that lit
the observatory plate took
that light-year-distance long
to reveal sixty-million-billion
miles of shooting suns!
                    How strange
the illusion runs, (how time tangles
in the vast), that our today
is blind but to the universe's past.

Beyond such speed-time limits
we need breakthrough-mind—
                    science-intuitions—
to find that the galactic
past our instruments show
is not all we have
of universe, nor all we know.

FOR THE HAVING: THE SERMON ON THE MOUNT

Following that incisive summation
                              en-fold of brother love
of spiritual cause/spiritual effect
                              windowed release to law
the people saw
that Jesus "taught them as one having authority,
and not as the scribes"—

    (the scribes who demanded
    but practiced not,
    who claimed to be authority
    and therefore law to others,

        self-lifting to the upper rooms
        self-rewarding with the enlarged borders).

Hearts turned, stirred
incandescent with hope that lit the centuries quick with healing
through Jesus' impeccable practice
                              of having authority.
     Oh veilless equity, emancipating men to mercy

He who loved the having of Love's authority, taught others their having
                    through prayer:
                    that difficult, single-eyed task
                              of yielding
                    in unlabored reflection
                    to God's knowable allness.
Striking down the un-healing
              the tyranny of scribal pride and push to hold off heaven,
Jesus said, and did: Principle's way: un-selfing mortality,
                         enlightening, and letting
                         our everywhere-at-once-present
                         Father
                         lift His unsmug children
                                        us, too! us, too!
into unboundaried perception
                    and harmony for the having.

BY THESE

On a morning
When small things count
Like neatness

On household rounds I note
Visitors mounting
Door and screen and sill:

A praying mantis stick-still
And all green alert
Clings antennas-down
To a window screen,
Ultra-angular, precisely poised,
Eyes science-fiction celled
And extra-planetary clear;
        Why, hello there
        (Long wonder-stare)

Soft below
At the inside pane
A miller moth suns
His feathered feelers,
His stain of earthy-brown
And soot-soft wings;
> My heart sings
> Of common things

And at the door where hang
Five ears of Indian corn, a mouse
Comes borne by hunger-flaring need
To wrench away a colored seed. Fast!
Almost not seen. But seen. Known
As sleekly pink of paw,
Plush gray speed,
And awesome obsidian
Dot eyes, hard
With extremity of dare.
> No hurry, dear
> It is all to share

By these small encounters I duly note strange beauty,
A lilting contentment,
And a creature ness of care.
> All marked here
> Important and rare

ZINNIA-LINGUAL AT LAST

A side trip wasn't on the docket. My pocket
held the one-two-three schedule for a day
which brooked no delay. But before the way
closed to the open country I nosed
the car forward and left my turn behind—
sped straight ahead free to find
a farm-fresh vegetable stand. (The day's
strict demand was broken, seemed easier
to fulfill, and a token of trust.)
                    Dill weeds and dust;
chickens with their feathers mussed
in the south-blowing wind; hot blue glory-morning
sky; barbed wire fences shimmered by. And then
                    those zinnias.
A sturdy bunch had missed the yard somehow—
escaped the plow-planting by house and fence—
and lined the road, blown into emphatic nods
of approval at every outbound car. They crowded
so against the street, it was as though
their next move should be to see if they
could catch a ride to travel far and fleet.
There was nothing trivial about their welcome:
eager and poised, their convivial shouts of color
noised about the countryside good mornings of orange,
a red hello, purple yoo-hoos, and cheers of yellow.
                    Their hues cried
approbation into my day in such anticipation that
I answered back, with not one color lost in translation:
                    It appears
it was our mutual truancy
that delighted me into fluency
after all these years.

SOMETHING ABOUT CHILDREN

They inspire awareness
of what we all ever are:
children: open as teacups,
head-on as summer,
resilient as grass, sure
of possibilities, glad
for now; alarmed
sometimes by what might be
of vagaries beyond seeing,
reassured by a word, a touch,
by stars, by sun, by much to love
and read and make and do
in proof of being.

FOR THE FAMILY

Three dandelions,
one tiny
and three minuscule
flowers
are offered by a child
sure of the magnificence
of her gift.

and with her hours
under the whole
broad, blue sky
lifting in her eyes.

The bouquet
won't make
much of a show,
barely above the rim
of our smallest vase.
Just a small glow
of color, and gay.

And we know the singing
space, the open-curling miles
of meadows and lark-
spanned fields she is bringing
with that handful of blossoms
and her smile.

VACATION FIND

Delight-bright child,
peripheral explorer
at the ocean's mild
edge, halfway between
tides you run swift above
your sea-thin reflection;
gladness—transparent love
for this day's lambent
embrace of protection—
has given you hover-craft speed,
(while I am open-stilled
at this guaranteed glimpse of
child-essence affection).

SOME ESSENTIALS

Off to school, small
daughter ran bang out the door
after the everyday kiss goodbye
and wave; morning duties began,
young son hummed over his play,
and the shutter was swung open
      to welcome the view
of neighborhood trees branched black
against a pewter sky and the new
day's activity of weather.
      Whether delayed
by diversion or by need,
there they were, instant-stayed
in speed, child and child,
yours and mine, through the window
framed winter-bright, feet flying
over the eggshell grass, ballerinas
bundled against the cold,
holding lunch sacks, hugging books,
run-twirling, all plaid sparkle,
all glad togethering! Their scarves
flipped up over flower-stem necks, above
sun-silk hair, exclamation points
to their joy. As much lift-up
as push-forward to their going,
spindle-legs blurred, angled
knees camera-caught in foal-like grace
on a lacework day, splash and play
of tint, line, and light.
The happy chase caught up everything!

Birds and squirrels joined
in flight and frisk
peripheral to their whirl-winding path
       of purpose.

That child-simple moment let me see
       some essentials
about art, what music is made of, and poetry.

CONGRUITY

He came running
    on elation's stilts,
towering almost too much
    for the ceiling,
to tilt with me who might say no
    from far below his want-to feeling.
"Can I....?" No question, really.
    Urging—out of deeps of held-in
joy. I stand quiet seconds' stern watch
    for a right decision. "Yes!"

Stilts turn
    to action-springs of glad song-steel;
he boy-bounds on to the special play
    and we part, acknowledging smiles
that open-say, heart to heart,

I know how you feel!/You know how I feel!

SUMMER CIRCUS

**A Documentary: For Moms and Dads and Children
of All Ages, in Spite of Some Big Words**

(To be read aloud with conversational theatricality)

A circus was being whispered through the house—
A circus so special I would be a mouse
To hear the plans and see young eyes go bright
When they hit on the parts and players just right.
Whisper, giggle, disagree,
Whisper, giggle, One, two, Three
Little girls sprouting ideas for an ex-TRAV
A-ganza as wonderful as any real circuses have:

>   the six-year-old would walk a rope;
>   and they could beard a "lady" with shaving soap;
>   there would be a lion tamer to tame
>   the smallest boy in the circus game;
>   the little brothers could each by a clown—
>   they'd need no practice in falling down
>   and getting laughs; there would also be
>   a specialty act about a flea,
>   and a breathtaking cowboy and Indian drama;
>   and, hey! How about cookies from somebody's mama?
>   and popcorn, and music; oh, yes! and lights,
>   and ballons, and costumes, and pink satin tights.

The mouse tiptoed out to sweep the floors,
But two days later in neighborhood doors
There were handmade flyers of red and white

> ANNOUNCING
>
> A CIRCUS AT 8 TONIGHT!

45

Summer days have a way of going long with reason:
At seven fifty-six the unseasoned
Troupe wasn't very ready.
One was still eating spaghetti
From supper time,
And one was lost on a tall-tree climb.
When an eager audience began to arrive
They formed a crew of five
Unplanned circus hands. A good thing, too!
The show could start *almost* on cue.
A single ring circled the encircling trees
(Made of pink crepe paper if you please!)
And a phonograph played
And stirred the children to parade—
High feelings, and a hullabaloo
Of claps and whistles. Then a silence grew.

AND...

        the tightrope walker in a pink tutu
        walked the next-door fence
        all pointy-toed and balanced tense
        as a thistle of swept child-grace;
        the bearded lady took her place
        in the center of the ring with the aplomb of a pro
        and told her short, sad tale of woe.

A ROLL OF DRUMS! TA-DAA! "AND NOW..."

        the cowboy-Indian saga, with a grandiloquent bow
        by the Only One to Survive! For a change of pace,
        a single comic and her tricky flea,

then a long, blank space while
the clowns were found for their jubilee
act. The tamer tamed his beast (a bobcat skin
covered the grin
of a small but lion-voiced lad),
and then,
the best songs-and-somersaults finale a circus ever had!

I was so GLAD
To have been a mouse
And heard those plans whispered about the house,
Seen the way their bigtop intentions grew
Without a tangible resource in sight;
Here were the results of pure WANTING - TO—
A full-blown, real-live circus, all right!
Thin on props, full of élan,
The wonderful, show-magic phenomenon
Of dares and scares fraught
With fun had been wrought
by clowns that made the audience squeal,
performers that brought peal after peal
of applause,
a lion as real as though BORN with claws,
And delicious laughter
That lasted long after
Goodnights were said
And the last balloon sailed moonward,
And we went happy-home to bed!

SUMMER CIRCUS

A Documentary: For Moms and Dads
And Children of All Ages, In Spite of Some Big Words

(To be read aloud with conversational theatricality)

A circus was being whispered through the house--
A circus so special I would be a mouse
To hear the plans and see young eyes go bright
When they hit on the parts and players just right.
Whisper, giggle, disagree,
Whisper, giggle. One two, three
Little girls sprouting ideas for an ex-TRAV-
A-ganza as wonderful as any real circuses have:

    the six year old would walk a rope;
    and they could beard a "lady" with shaving soap;
    there would be a lion tamer to tame
    the smallest boy in the circus game;
    the little brothers could each be a clown--
    they'd need no practice in falling down
    and getting laughs; there would also be
    a specialty act about a flea,
    and a breathtaking cowboy and Indian drama;
    and, hey! how about cookies from somebody's mama?
    and popcorn, and music; oh, yes! and lights,
    and balloons, and costumes, and pink satin tights..

The mouse tiptoed out to sweep the floors,
But two days later in neighborhood doors
There were handmade flyers of red and white

      ANNOUNCING

    A CIRCUS AT 8 TONIGHT!

Summer days have a way of going long with reason:
At seven fifty-six the unseasoned
Troupe wasn't very ready.
One was still eating spagetti
From supper time,
And one was lost on a tall-tree climb.
When an eager audience began to arrive
They formed a crew of five
Unplanned circus hands. A good thing, too!
The show could start almost on cue.
A single ring circled the encircling trees
(Made of pink crepe paper, if you please!)
And a phonograph played
And stirred the children to parade--
High feelings, and a hullabaloo
Of claps and whistles. Then, a silence grew.

AND...

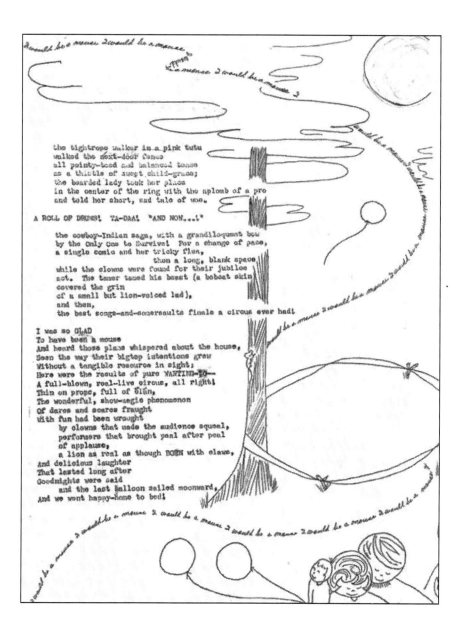

the tightrope walker in a pink tutu
walked the next-door femme
all pointy-toed and balanced tense
as a thistle of swept child-grace;
the bearded lady took her place
in the center of the ring with the aplomb of a pro
and told her short, sad tale of woe.

A ROLL OF DRUMS! TA-DAA! "AND NOW...!"

the cowboy-Indian saga, with a grandiloquent bow
by the Only One to Survive! For a change of pace,
a single comic and her tricky flea,
                    then a long, blank space
while the clowns were found for their jubilee
act. The tamer tamed his beast (a bobcat skin
covered the grin
of a small but lion-voiced lad),
and then,
the best songs-and-somersaults finale a circus ever had!

I was so GLAD
To have been a mouse
And heard those plans whispered about the house,
Seen the way their bigtop intentions grew
Without a tangible resource in sight;
Here were the results of pure WANTING-TO—
A full-blown, real-live circus, all right!
Thin on props, full of élan,
The wonderful, show-magic phenomenon
Of dares and scares fraught
With fun had been wrought
          by clowns that made the audience squeal,
          performers that brought peal after peal
          of applause,
          a lion as real as though BORN with claws,
And delicious laughter
That lasted long after
Goodnights were said
          and the last balloon sailed moonward,
And we went happy-home to bed!

49

A WONDERMENT

"I like all this QUIET!"
—a child's pronouncement.

There can be a quiet of home
that is not the absence of sound
but full stillness.
    Unenclosed
by word or note or sound,
    silence
says something of
empowered serenity
and sings through the house
a penetration of openness
that embraces us in daytime stars
and people-shine, and
    small-voice call.

A child and I found the quiet
of home today as tangible,
more lovely, than the Taj Mahal.

BOY-WATCHING, DEEPLY

The earth was fine! and his! He always
knew it, and at age two, told me so
as he leaned from my arms with his own outstretched
and declared, "Mine!"
                              True. But not the mine/grab
of possession—the mine/give of dominion:
giving the mountains his awe, the day his glee,
the sunshine, beetle, and ant his wonder and oneness.

From my arms he climbed air like a column, rappelled
a solemn sky, recognized rainbows, scrambled
down. Sinew, muscle, bone, thew:
he was responsive all the way through to *belongingness*.

He still seeks contact of indivisibility:
discovers the gopher a blaze of truthful eyes,
the bird a stroke of earthlessness, the turtle's
tread a patience, a surprise of silence the snake's
scaled head; holds geometry in a geode
and accepts the dark inside the earth as un-
scary; finds the bear a sovereign presence,
a forgiveness the ginkgo tree, the trout a watersong
floated newly from an antiquity of sea.

And his, all his—the quest, the comprehending!

This boy crests earth not as colossus
but as confederate—in non-stop interest,
with level-look regard. He celebrates
the immanence of creation and his own createdness.
He grasps secrets of significance: the way
the earth holds rainbows to its core,
and rainbows spangle its sky and lie undulating
in its fishy waters and in every caring eye.

THE CLIMBER

The years of campers had left troughed paths
lined concave with the fragrant spines
of great-armed pines above. The boy, as new
to mountain walking as the morning was new
to itself, saw the path and followed it
by taking stones and boulders
at either side. It seemed he had to test
his sturdy step against the rocks and feel
the shocks of teetering against the next unknown,
had to know the hummingbird moment of poise
before the noise of sliding pebbles behind
urged the forward stride. Mountain-touched,
he went jubilant through the woods and sure,
finding stone-strength and boulder-balance.

He saw the path and followed it by taking
to the stones and boulders on either side.
The rocks were challenge, the needled path was guide.

IN PROOF

Children, open as teacups,

head-on as summer,

inspire awareness

of what we all ever are:

children: resilient as grass, sure

of possibilities, glad

for now; alarmed

sometimes by what might be

of vagaries beyond seeing,

reassured by a word, a touch,

by stars, by sun, by much to love

and read and make and do

in proof of being.

CHILDREN TRYING OUT BIKES, KITES, SKATES, BOOKS

Their learning looks
awkward—

gangly, scrawny,
scraggly, brawny.

They laugh at themselves, each other.

Their faces make funny-
faces, bodies contort, flail
about, tump over, recover.

Their learning looks
awkward—goofiness of joy
is contagious.
I also laugh,

simultaneous with
a ride of heart
stirred certain
that their striving

is the hug of wholeness,
the tough weathering-through
of prodigy.

THESE CHILDREN

New like colts
to first-summer clouds, children
bolt about wanting rain,
put on suits to catch showers in,
kick up glad heels waiting under
          peals of thunder
for rain to pour, sniff the water-
settled dust fragrant from the south,
they soar, and call across the lawns,
          anticipating.

First small drops
are caught on upturned faces, outstretched
arms, then torrents take them by expected
surprise, and they kick their traces—
dance delight, puddle-splash, outleap
the frogs, shelter shouting under trees.

These children laugh
at the pavement-plops that look
as though the water came from there
          and was falling up,
and at their wet-maned reflections—in love
with all their shining world watered
          fresh from heaven's cup!

OUR SECRET VISITOR

When the light
 is just right,
  when there is little at all,
   at twilight, say,
    or in the bright-skied glow
     of a summer night,
      or when the lightning lifts the unmooned dark
       of the early fall to show,
        what's there,
         there lumbers up from the woods behind
          yes! a dinosaur! He stands
           with his head and neck arched high
            against the city sky,
             great body and slow tail in among the oaks.
              Ssh! It's the best hackberry tree in our yard
               that he is after, we have guessed,
                with the good ginkgo for dessert.
                 He looks this way, moving back and forth now,
                  in a gentle, cumbersome quandry
                   of how to step over
                    the split-rail fence, and under
                     the strangeness
                      of telephone wires
                       all through starshine, and sunglow, and rain.
                        He belongs to us now, like Pooh Bear endeared
                         by his very little brain;
                          he is part of the family, one of the folks,
                           made as he is, of imagination-in-oaks!

When the light
is just right,
when there is little at all,
at twilight, say,
or in the bright-shied glow
of a summer night,
or when the lightning lifts the unsecond dark
of the early fall to show
what's there,
there lumbers up from the woods behind
just a dinosaur! He stands
with his head and neck arched high
against the city sky,
great body and slow tail in among the oaks.
Sssh! It's the best hackberry tree in our yard
that he is after, we have guessed,
with the good gingko for dessert.
He looks this way, moving back and forth and
in a gentle, cumbersome quandry
of how to step over
the split-rail fence and under
the strangeness
of telephone wires
all through starshine, and sunglow, and rain.
He belongs to us now, like Noah ever endeared
by his very little brain;
he is part of the family, one of the folks,
made as he is, of imagination-in-oaks!

57

PRINCESS SCRUFFYSIX,
MEET PRINCESS MELLOWTWELVE

Princess Scruffysix
   talks teetertotters,
tells diamond-dust certainties,
   uses body English all bounce
with hopscotch hosannas,
   basks expansively
in the lap of being listened to
   deeply, and learns from largess.

Princess Mellowtwelve
   looks cameras,
listens sponges of approval,
   harnesses winged laughter
to sedate delight in this darling
   petaling of kinetic news,
is surprised to discover her own
   so-very-recent past.

They revel in their royal hour, their vast
   kingdom in common, and their diverse dower.

FIRST MENDING

Sewing under the day's-end lamp
in contentment's ringing silence,
the child is a study of flower-petal
fingers and sunshine head.
          A gingerly care
works at the prickly needle, the tangly
          thread. And I wish her
to look up from that delicate struggle,
from that nimbus of earnest girl-grace.

          I wish her
to look up, not as the cat wills one
to open the window and let him in,
          but as an observer
who sees something of much moment
and wants to share. I wish for her
          to look up and see
          something of good
has been understood, and is loved.

LITTLER THAN LITTLE LEAGUE

The boy who came to play
　　and waited for someone to say
　　the magic words

hid the baseball glove behind
　　his back, and covered it with a kind
　　of shy smile that invited invitations.

So his friend said, "Want to play
　　baseball?" and the boy with the smile
　　intensified with more

smile than could be accounted for
　　in one so small, and threw
　　the hidden glove and his smile

heavenward to signify a yes a mile
　　too high for hallelujah,
　　and caught it all to him with a hug.

IN FROM OUTSIDE

The child
whose tendrilous
still warmly steams
with her fervor
for running air
a race
breathes mild exultations
and sits wrapped
in the embrace
of wonder: *lift is lovely;*
speed is one's own thrust
of belonging, and trust.

Her collar rides askew, all grace
below the rosy, lucent
face; in the clarity of her eyes
one sees science fiction-facts balloon:
from hints, she draws intensities
and dreams of giant-jumping on the moon.

CALM-TOLD

He ran from home at the owl's inviting call,
stayed not by the garden wall or sandpile swing,
but ran to where the birds, exuberant, sing
morning-burst gladness within the woodsy mall.

Through the brambled arcs of shadow and shine
the anxious mother followed to seek the tiny
truant and called to him as sharply as the stickered vine
at first, but then as softly as the owlet, fluent
with persuasion, when the red of a baby bird, bright
through the arching arms of leaf-luminous trees
and the blue practice of a young jay's wobbly flight
calm-told her that the woods embowering these
held nothing uncared for, no harmful plight,
and was safe shelter for her child's spring delight.

MEASURE OF TIME

"Sorry I got to supper late.
Our team....we won!"

"That's all right, son."
No need to explain:
no gap, no strain

between you-of-the-shared-home,
the we-young-once;

and no need to scold
when free runs the flow
        of what we see by indirection
        by unintention know.

        Symbols say it:

grass and leaves cling to your shirt
        like medals
for heroic companioning,
and you are mantled in the manliness
of gratitude for game and team;

recognition smiles, and we are crowned
        with laurels
of love; we approve
the measure of time by joy, glad
there is no need to clock-watch the years
        or this boy.

CHILD AT THE SEASHORE

Is this your first visit
to the elliptical world
of sea-stretched island?
Your exultant sand-sprint
proclaims your delight in this place
of crystalline color and curved space.

You stop (surely not
at being fenced in or out)
to wonder
at finding you have already won
the horizon's there
in this moment's now,
and so—no need to run.

(Small discoverer, and silent
like Keats' Cortez,
hearing from some inward peak
what the heart's-chord says.)

OH BEAUTIFUL!

The vacation begins—our four-
wheeled ark leaves
the sleeping familiar behind
in the predawn dark.

The sun wakes new a world
horizon to horizon flat,
giving the domed sky
full play of arch,
early hot and blue,
and horizon to horizon full
of ripe-grown wheat,
its hues soft and bright,
and shimmering canary-warm
to where the earth curves out of sight.
The horizon shortens into hill
and the car swings hillward up
to let the highway through
yellow into the green and blue
of sage under mesas and mesquite;
pale sands show
dry and hard, and over
this land, under each bluff,
cattle are browsing out
the tender from the tough.

On either side windmills
spin, exclamatory-tall;
on the south, the soft earth
into farmer's yellow spills;
on the north, the rancher's
rough-hunched hills,
under the sun that countenances all.

WE'RE COMING, HOUSE

House, we're coming home,
and bringing you something
from our roam through summer days—
    bouquets
for your each room
fresh from our grateful-eyed zoom
across other states:
from a pine-sheltered canyon
    (to nod above the breakfast plates)
we carry stream-sung columbine
and the rain-hung grace of clematis vine;
gathered from under a full scoop of sky
    (for the children's rooms of sleep and play)
poppies from the plains, and a pink nosegay
of verbenas to remember the desert by;
    the den will hold the yucca's spike
dug on an arid, sand-burned hike
and planted in a Mexican pot
to remind our wintered hours of hot
mesas and mesquite lands
giving sage and flowers from sucked-dry sands;
    the living room gets the largest one—
from a mountain meadow
high-swung below an aspened sun,
armfuls of larkspur and native rose,
scarlet gilia, and the meditative pose
of purple monkshood; cranesbill and
primrose and painted cup
    will fill up tomorrow
    with this trip's today.
So House, get ready! We're coming gay—
full of lovely things to tide us over
the winter's work with summer's clover.

BURNING BUSH

There is a bush
　　　that grows behind the house
　　　that seems just the kind
　　　　　　on which birds of a feather
　　　　　　like to get together.

It is a bush
　　　that grows from center
　　　up and out, easy to enter
　　　　　　for a flock of sparrows
　　　　　　or a shock of cardinals.

Brotherly,
they sit in unison,
　　　a conflagration
　　　twitting thanks
　　　　　　for what was found at the feeder-banks
　　　　　　of crumbs and seed.

A winter bush
　　　that smolders with sparrows
　　　and kindles with cardinals
　　　　　　turns me aside to heed
　　　　　　its fountained fire: I stand
　　　　　　entranced before the graceful blaze
　　　　　　of a lyric, incandescent praise!

DAY IN MIDSUMMMER

This still day,

catching everything in its cooler

light, cannot pass uncommemorated

into moon-washed night.

It must be remembered

for giving respite from July

heat and summer-strong winds

with the unstinting gentleness

of sweet and perfect weather.

Not a feather

ruffled, not a jay's fuss rent

the day; the neighborhood children

in have-at-it play hung the air

with happy calls and fair flew

the work, with window-stalls open

to the tender sky sprung burnt-blue

above the morning lines of fresh-hung

wash; the honeysuckle vines hummed

full-sigh with bees, and the doors swung

often open behind the young

pleased to bring the outside in. Spin

on earth, we happy urge, to an afternoon

festooned with summer-soft sun

showering quiet beauty, and deep

in spangled leaf and petal.

Oh let duty keep

pace with the day's light touch

crowning every face, each blade of grass.

Oh let us make much of such a day,

and do not let it pass

without the salute of an evening song

in glad psalm-tone

for the revolution now leaving lovely,

and we some taller grown.

WHAT IS THERE ABOUT PIGS AT THE STATE FAIR THAT IS LIKE A W.C. FIELDS' MOVIE?

Assertive creatures, these pigs with cardboard ears,
jar-lid snouts and shouts too shrill
to be heard as anything but silly screams.
Their pointy, cleft hoofs are too-dainty
support for the heft above, so
they run prissy-chop and their ear tips
flop incongruously. They eat exuberant, celebratory
meals, all noise and trough-plow.

We fence-lean, observe: those surprise-pink
hides, that scattering of truculent bristles briskly
vulnerable; country-gentlemen jowls; those incised
smiles; all that guttural garrulousness;
those teensy eyes and tics of distrust; that grace
of solid-centered rotundity, bolt-action quick.
We laugh at the ludicrous.

                  Three pigs in a pen
sight a fellow trotter being urged squealing
toward the show ring by a 4-H boy. They rally up
excitement, capsize as they charge the gate,
shriek arduously and overly, wreak an electric
havoc through the barn. Children grand-gesture covering
their ears. Business-as-usual for pigs and handlers.
We laugh at pigs on the outside, at ourselves
within, recognizing all-out panic in a pigpen
when we see it as funny, endearingly funny.

In a farther pen, the pigs rush a Future
Farmer of America bearing two pails of feed,
turn him heels up and over in a swirl
of flying grains. "Oh, they didn't mean it,"
he explains to us alarmed. "They're just hungry."

And intensely enthusiastic, those unpicky porkers,
intelligent Yorkshires, Durocs, Poland Chinas;
characters of nursery rime fame and science
fiction; of scrutable Eastern origin, domesticated
out of ancient forests; mud their comfort;
truffles their affinity; obsession of Lord Emsworth
of Blandings; nicely preferring cleanliness
next to hogliness; power- motored with contentment;
Piglet-y unsure; suffused with quivering hysteria;
packed with opinions and declaring them sans restraint,
avec vigor; concentrations of awareness and response;
sensitive learners; and so perpetually replete
with whole-hog action their tails are curlycues
of pent-up energy, whirligig semaphores,
curled whirly with drama-at-the-ready.

We leave the barn. The sky burns cool
autumn blue; the fairgrounds' chrysanthemums catch
the light like silent laughter free from distortion.
I get it then: from paradox, proportion.

GOOD OFFICES

The new fence is up. The dratted, dreaded,

Vertical-slatted fence. It shines too

Bright in the morning light, too new and raw

And wrong. The woods behind, the weathered cottage,

Were kind to eye and storybook-food for us.

But this stop-all fence! A fuss of new

Yellow lumber that says, "Spiked Fences

Make Prickly Neighbors;" yes, and, "Stay Away,"

And, "Ours, Not Yours." Well, there is nothing

That lures bushes and birds and vines like a fence.

It won't take long. Months hence

Third-party nature will have made its claims,

And resolved fence and feelings into larger aims.

PERSPECTIVE

"I love this new world!"
-from a letter by an American
student studying and traveling
in Europe

Who says

there is a dearth

of earth's frontiers?

For this girl

in whom meekness is lord:

new *light* is new *world*.

AT LAST

For once
April's cruelty
of youth and newness
comes as a kindness

its intensity tempered
to a lift of melody
that leaves the heart

untroubled;

less a passion
than a gladness

not so much a suddenness
as a continuity,

as if some tensile stirring
of the year's primeval hum
came comfortably into song.

KIPLING NOTWITHSTANDING

It is your turn, China,
to tilt from sun; you can stargaze
soon and let the lilting moon shine
reflective rest, while we head
sunward to celebrate the day's
quick-time zest. The earth's revolution
toward the set center of our system
quiets your day, quells our night.
Dawn never seemed so welcome, movement
toward the midmost light and certain
warmth so playful. Our sunrise a east,
your sunset west
                meet,
the cosmos in common. We all bask daily,
as now, in this undividable,
sane and simple, neat, disclosing glow.

CYCLE

Windmills—
Turning slowly
In a passing zephyr
Against a warm blue sky.

Windmills—
Going faster,
Fanned by a rising breeze
From out a sky of thunderheads.

Windmills—
Winding quickly
In a boisterous gale
Against dark and portentous clouds.

Windmills—
Turning slowly
In a passing zephyr
Against a warm blue sky.

Moore High School
Age 17

THIS FOLD

What is this? this round
of days and duties, this smallness of shepherding
that soothes away wooly wounds at noon,
that attends every midnight stray?

and what this? this strength
to lean upon, this
through-and-through care
that upholds wholeness,
that unfolds shepherd and enfolds sheep?

This round, this strength, this fold of sheep

is the spiral turn toward heaven,
what heaven owns, the watch we keep.

LAMBENT AS A FLAME

she rose
before the morning light
to do her part
for the day to come
all Christmas-true.

The house to warm
with fragrance,
the table to lay,
shining thoughts
and prayers to say
were hers
before the others woke.

The tree lights
spoke singing,
and the windowed dark
betokened the certain spark
of the morning star
in all its continuity.

She worked gently
so as not to mar
expectation
and Christmas perpetuity.

TO MEASURE A FIELD

A fence can measure a field
post by post, and
wire-by-foot-by-mile;
and the eye can compass
the open land to the horizon's
smile of grass or hill or tree.

But there is a measure
surer than survey,
fuller than eye can see:

we mark a meadow
by a span of heart
and a meadowlark's song,
and know the land as dearly more
than merely wide and long.

KITCHEN CONCERT

The noonday concert swirls Mahler's Seventh
about the house and through the doors,
                sings to me
of this day's intensity of beauty
and lifts the chores to exercises of elegance,
cadenza deeds with broom and mop.
The lyricism moves as I move, and I with it,
in the music's clear circle
                of unsealed timelessness.

Apples are peeled at the sunny window
                in the wash of melody
lit by B-minor strings and brass
to full-color roundness (and petaled trees
image-bloom about me and bend to spring);
the pastry is rolled out
under a tympani tumult, the edges
fluted fancy to the curling rhythms
of song and dance,
                while I inward sing
                that apple pie and symphony
make high romance.

REAPPRAISAL: BEYOND 180 X 360

A fence may mark a field post by post,

and wire by foot by mile. The eye can compass

the open land to the horizon's earthcurve smile

of hill or tree. But there is a measure

surer than survey, truer than transit or eye

can see: reckon a meadow

                        as a galaxy's home

for blackeyed Susan, bumblebee, rabbits'

nest, milkweed, mole, bobwhite

quail, for the meadowlark's sky-hung, boundless,

whole-notes song—and hail the land

as dearly more than merely wide and long!

CLOSE ABOUT

Summer's woods
are dense about the house;
    no neighbors' lights
    show through, nor star nor sky;
but leafy sun and shade
shelter owl, possum and turtle,
nest the squirrel and those that fly
    and these make good neighbors.
    We hear their calls,
    watch progeny grow,
    see shelled house
    by violets moving slow;
fireflies' flickers make woods
    star zone,
and those sky-thing birds seem
    our very own!

AFTERNOON OUT

Nature sings me
praiseful lessons: companioning
with an afternoon of tree-stretch,
             water-glint,
             impartial sky,
reminds the jaded eye and heart
that this moment is
a foreverness free
of used-to-be, of not-yet,
a rightness and certainty of *now*,
real as an airplane, warm
             as a cow.

                 Let columbines
and birch, spider and gnat,
a far-off barking dog,
the sunning cat,
be friends to my afternoon out,
and I doubt not that infinitesimals
have their ordered place and mooring
in the graces of nature's outpouring—
and that all things simply be
out of some great and good necessity.

BREAKTHROUGH

We watched with water-austere
eyes a red-tailed hawk break through
our skies and make a lambent line
in the barren blue above last year's
fallowed grasses. He must have liked
the land's plain lay—he wheeled
and hung, and plunged his way to earth,
stirred the dust and whirred upward
again in rust-winging, clear hieroglyphs
of uncontested dominion.

My opinion of the view of green-gone
longing and monochrome sleep changed
to hold indelible that sweep and fling
of glad and bold belonging that made
the heavens a singing hue, the heart
to catch on spring!

HARK! THE HARVEST HERALDS SING

Toward the sun the day goes
and pulls everything with it—
petals, paperboys, sleepyhead
children, grown-already-ups,
autumn itself, and sky, sky, sky!

Crickets sing out night
in the dark beneath the shrubs
even while the dawn vaults
white above. We who slept under
zephyr sheets and serenade
wake on the run into a day brimming day
burdenless and beckoning.

One cricket's sticky chirp lasts long
after our rising, is louder
than footsteps, faucets, drawer thumpshuts,
louder than teakettle song,
silver-on-pottery clatter,
morning talk, and goodbyes.

We cherish each other away
under layered skies that harbinger harvests,
past light-blurred blossoms and hedges
into open-eyed traffic, and on
to companion with enterprise.

The day is ours, for each and all—
proved by our participation,
and steady with cricket-cheer elation.

LENS

apple tree wet
is apple tree new

dry-brown bark
transforms to

distinguished
green, seen

striated yellow-
green and thin

of skin; image
of green-grow

through and through
and marvelous.

apple tree wet
is apple tree new

new leaves amove
with light, with rain

and hanging drops
tops and tips ashine

rain under thunder
newness under rain

mine the wonder
of seeing plain

bole and branch
every leaf

bud, twig
stick, stalk

vein and view
new!

AFTER RAIN

Through the kitchen window I see
the rain is over. On the sill
the floating comb in the honey jar
is cut through with moistened light;
outside, a rainbow stretch defines
itself twice—muted, and bright—
while a water-glad boy in slickered glee
shakes down more showers from a willing tree.

On the pane, rain-round crystal drops
(so summer-soon dried up) enfold the moment
multiplied—catch the glow of boy and bow,
and hold them heaven side up!

A TUFT OF WORK

My broom soft-brushes through silent
rooms empty of family,
and on the walk outside
makes brisk noises
that ride upon the morning's hum
                    of beginnings.
The distant traffic
and children's playground voices
                    murmur, birds
trill song-signals
about nests and twine,
and the whine of a saw
hones the hearing high and cheering.
                    A milkman
whistles up the street and I greet
all these sounds of industry
as a grand companioning, a solace
of touch, a much-flowering mutuality.

RESUMÉ

My father is
a morning kind of man
    who loves
an instant, eager dawn
or the long, quiet coloring
    of a deliberate sun;
a morning kind of man, awake
to fellow creatures, to beast and bird,
and day-tuned to appreciate
every nuance of light,
every lift of leaf and flight
    of heart,
and intensely comfortable
    with challenge.

FEE-FIE-FO-FUM

I smell openness—
the sunlit, guileless
wonder of day
and clean skies
and a universe
where pollen, galaxies,
people, wooden spoons,
grasshoppers, mushrooms,
ellipses, super-novas,
mysteries, and apples
are held distinct, and
aromatic with equity.

GIFT: SUMMER

This is for every one of us
this pungent gratitude
the earth exudes
of universal weeds blossomed
tinypollened and warmpetaled,
upward filling tented arches
of world-over trees and blending
fragrances buoyant as smiles.

Broody skies curve earth, nurture
newness, melt holdback

and earth responds,
minion ever of the sun,
in great wind blown
birdflown exchanges
of people, waters, insects, seeds.

We take perennial turns
at summer's opening, its unowned
ungarnered, unchecked, burgeoning
beauty. It is elegantly ours,
a kind of laborless work
a kind of schoolless learning
a holiday benevolence in common—
active as balladeer bees, yielding
as orchards and wildflower fields.

CELEBRATE THE SURE THING

Something of perfection
is hinted here
in this day's shining
pace: its rhythm
is rising fall, filled
with the immediacy of love-
likeness in leaf
and butterfly space
and total tree.

We who also are
celebrate the sure thing
under the bird's fringed wing,
within the meek of child,
about the sky's mild intensity;
every home-being knows
there's not a war wind blows
that can bolt out or mar
this day-drop immensity.

COUNTERLESSON: DOMINION

"You will sit a little closer to me, every day."

So Saint-Exupery's Little Prince learned
a lesson from a fox about taming and being tamed:
it takes time, you know, and patience to train a friendship,
be a friend. Slow it seems and so daily
those rites practiced to established ties that the skies
bend down warm around them
before friend finally acknowledges friend.

Wildness eases, smiles, becomes unwild.

Until parting comes and tempts a whimper. Whimper
follows whimper and plunges untamed to want
to shriek and gnash and (willful) flail the air
with "No. You cannot go. I will not have it so."
But the howl tires before utterance, sinks
in upon itself, sobs silence
to the dust.

   Centered in quiet, the gentled heart
can survive the semblance of break, keep live the love,
unbroken the tiny trust.

   Then, in dissolve
of anguish, the jeweled reptile and the small-eyed
dew, the spill of rain, the hue of day
and sigh of grain in the greening wind—the whole
play of the year into daystar spring!—sing
distinctly of friendship's seasoning
     which discovers, beyond
reasoning, that the esteem practiced in being tamed to care
is crowning kindredness to everyone, everywhere.

ACKNOWLEDGMENTS

With grateful acknowledgment to the editors, many of the poems in this collection previously appeared in the following publications:

The Christian Science Monitor
1963: Child at the Seashore (6/22), Continuum (7/19), Zinnia-Lingual at Last (7/27), Vacation Find (8/21), Autumns Honors (9/6), We're Coming, House (9/16), Breakthrough (12/3), After Rain (12/5)
1964: The Climber (4/15), Oh Beautiful! (7/16)
1965: Day in Midsummer (7/6), Close About (7/7), The Greater (8/6), Kitchen Concert (12/8), Congruity
1967: A Wonderment (4/3), Fee-Fie-Fo-Fum (4/26), Welcome (5/19), Something About Children (5/26)
1968: Afternoon Out (2/24)
1970: Lens (3/26), In From Outside (4/18), By These (5/2), Neither X Nor Ice (10/23), Measure of Time (10/31)
1971: Burning Bush (3/17)
1974: Celebrate the Sure Thing (10/23),
1975: First Mending (1/21), Counterlesson: Dominion (5/8), Galaxies Observed (5/13)
1976: Gift: Summer (7/8)
1977: This Fold (12/13)
1978: Nature Qualitative (4/21)
1979: Beyond Winter (1/25)
1988: Princess Scruffysix, Meet Princess Mellowtwelve (1/6), Winter's Part (2/5), Letter of (Urgent) Recommendation (8/8)

The Christian Science Journal
July 1977: For the Having: The Sermon on the Mount

The Christian Science Sentinel
1963: The Stone the Builders Rejected (10/5)

Chelsea Magazine
1966: Discoveries: Galaxies and Electron Ringer

Good Housekeeping
1970: Joy Ride (3/19)

Hyacinths and Biscuits
1971: Joy Ride (Issue #4)

Kids, Etc.
1989: Our Secret Visitor, Summer Circus

Lawrence Eagle Tribune
1963: Child at the Seashore (6/28)

The Milory Farm Poetry Contest
1980: Small Town Girl (Honorable Mention; 4,727 entries)

The New Yorker
1979: What is There About Pigs at the State Fair That is Like a W. C. Field's Movie? (1/23)

The Ozarks Mountaineer
October 1964: Day Before Winter

Made in the USA
Columbia, SC
30 December 2020